Before the development of farming in the New Stone Age, man's life changed slowly and very little over thousands of years. But with farming, the pace of change quickened—changes that might have taken place over a thousand years, now occurred in one hundred years. Communities grew up in the Tigris-Euphrates Valley, where the need to irrigate the rich soil drew the first farmers together. Hamlets grew into villages, villages into cities.

Communal living brought new needs and possibilities for trade, taxation, and record keeping. City-dwellers worshipped a patron god who protected their city. A surplus of food freed architects and artisans to create temples for the gods. The temple, filled with intricately carved bowls, vases and tablets, was the center of city life. From simple beginnings, the Sumerian cities became the forerunners of the great modern metropolis.

Archeologists today continue to uncover more and more of Sumerian culture. Leonard Weisgard's pictures and text are faithfully based on their findings. THE BEGINNINGS OF CITIES is not only a valid conjecture on the way the early city-dwellers lived. It is a fascinating, vital glimpse of the past.

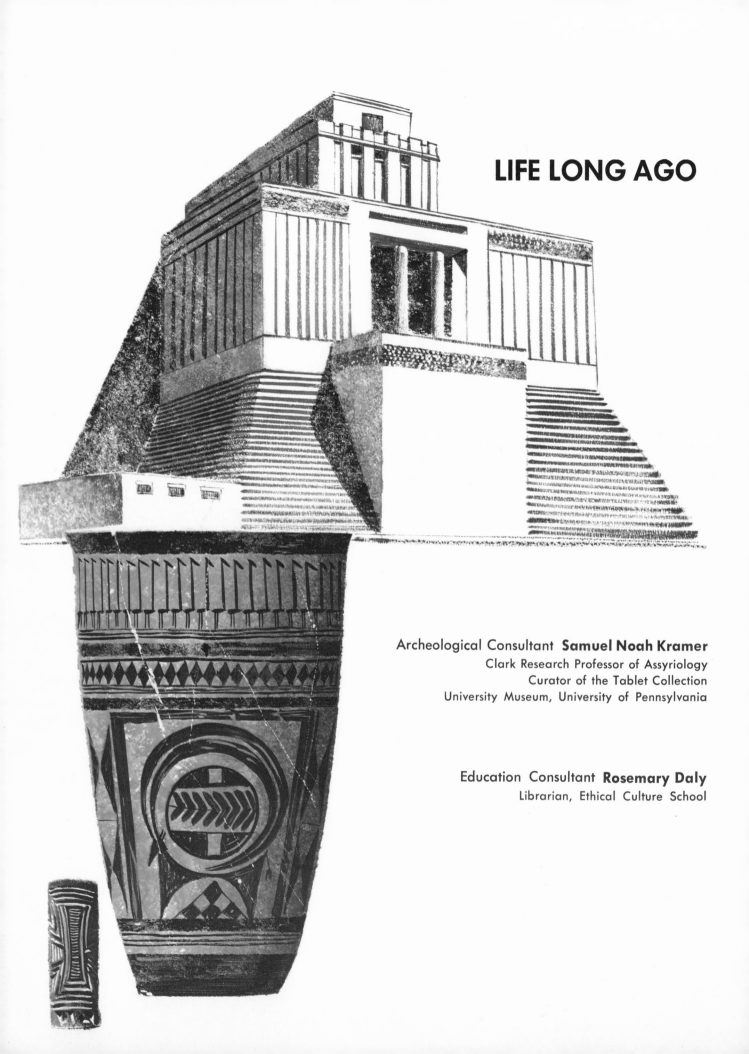

LIFE LONG AGO

Archeological Consultant **Samuel Noah Kramer**
Clark Research Professor of Assyriology
Curator of the Tablet Collection
University Museum, University of Pennsylvania

Education Consultant **Rosemary Daly**
Librarian, Ethical Culture School

THE BEGINNINGS
OF CITIES

RE-CREATION IN PICTURES AND TEXT OF MESOPOTAMIAN LIFE
FROM FARMING TO EARLY CITY BUILDING

LEONARD WEISGARD
author of THE FIRST FARMERS

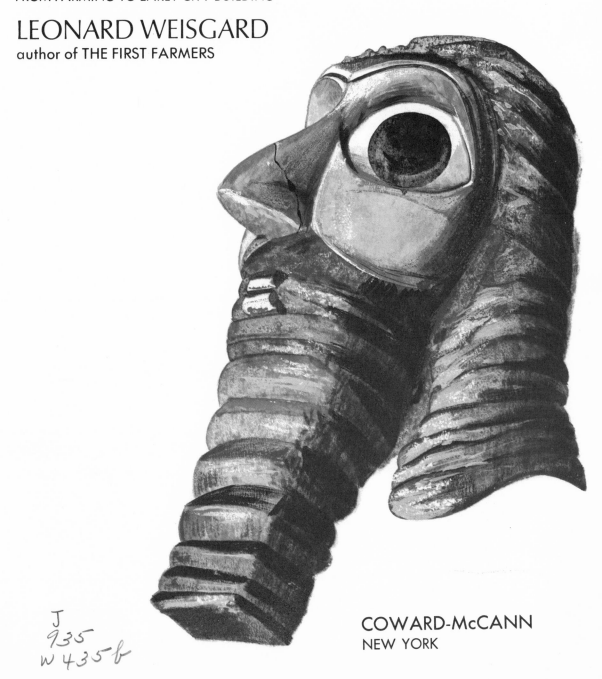

COWARD-McCANN
NEW YORK

Jacket:

Bas-relief from temple, al'Ubaid, about 2500 B.C.
Alabaster vase from temple, Uruk, about 3200 B.C.
Reconstruction of Ubaid temple, Tepe Gawra, about 3500 B.C.
Clay nail with cuneiform writing

Endsheet:

Ziggurat ruins, Aqar Quf, 1300-1200 B.C.

Title Page:

Temple reconstruction, Eridu, early Uruk period
Beaker, Susa, about 4000 B.C.
Cylinder seal, about 3000 B.C.
Head from statue, Abu temple, Tell Asmar

Half-title Page:

Bronze bull, height 7½ inches, Lagash, about 3000-2500 B.C.
Bowl, fired clay, diameter 11¼ inches, Tell-i-Bakun, about 4000 B.C.
Figure of priest, height 16 inches, Tell Asmar

Page 8:

Shard, Susa
Jar fragments, Samarra ware, Hassuna, 5000 B.C.
Account tablet, about 3200 B.C.

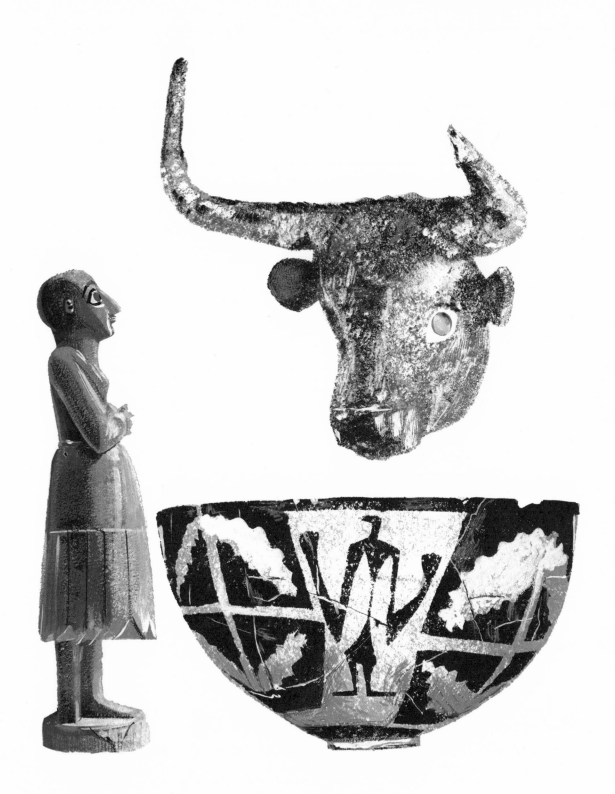

CONTENTS

HOW WE KNOW WHAT WE KNOW

Greek scholars and Old Testament Bible stories long ago told of Babylonians and Assyrians. They told of their rich flourishing cities in the land between the rivers of ancient Mesopotamia.

Thousands of years later, archaeologists began to dig for the remains of these cities. They found that one city had been built right on top of another. Each stood on the remains of an earlier settlement.

As the archaeologists dug deeper through layer under layer, they came upon unexpected finds. These were neither Babylonian nor Assyrian, not quite like either. Yet here was the evidence of a highly developed culture, the ruins of an impressive city. There was evidence of writing but no one could read it.

They continued to dig and to study. They found clay pieces with picture symbols which seemed to be writing but which they could not read. Who were the vanished people who had left them? The clues were there, but nobody yet knew how to decipher their meaning. Later, at the end of the last century, archaeologists learned that the city had been built and the records written by a people of whom they had never heard—the Sumerians.

At every level there was pottery, almost never unbroken, but the pieces were there in abundance. Clay pots break easily but can be pieced together.

These pots had distinct shapes and patterns. Some were turned on a wheel, some shaped by hand. Archaeologists gave to each type the name of the site where they first found it.

But pieces of the same type sometimes turned up far from that site. Archaeologists collected, labeled, pieced together and studied these countless clay remnants. They discovered bit by bit who had lived here and when. They learned much about trade and trade routes.

Still they were faced by a big gap between what was known of primitive hunters and food-gatherers and of the earliest settlements they had unearthed in southern Mesopotamia.

Southern Mesopotamia was barren in contrast to the foothills of the Zagros Mountains to the north, where grain grew wild. Robert J. Braidwood of the University of Chicago believed that digging there would unearth remains of the earliest farming settlements. These would yield clues of man's step-by-step progress from the beginning of farming to the culture of rich and powerful cities.

Digs in the Zagros foothills, first at Jarmo and a little later at Karim Shahir, pushed our knowledge of settled communities back from around 4500 B.C.—the earliest known settlements in southern Mesopotamia—to about 9000 B.C.

A diagrammatic cross section of a step trench excavation

of an archaeological dig at any Near Eastern mound.

Here, layer under layer, thousands of years of historic

and prehistoric cultures lie buried. By checking objects

found at each level, archaeologists can identify the time

and the people who made up the community at that place.

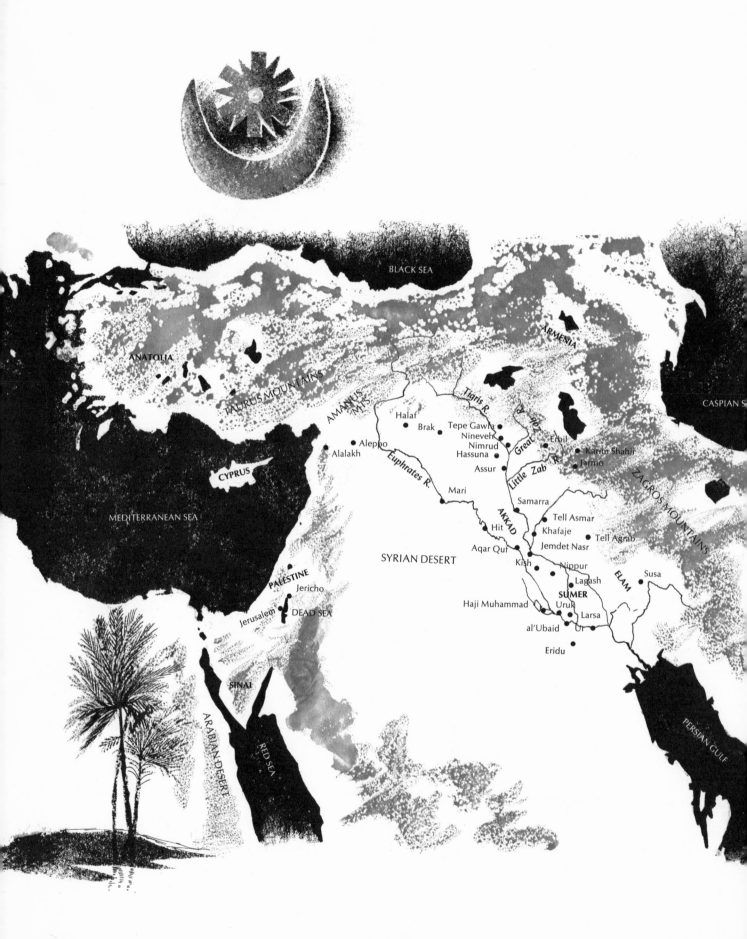

BLACK SEA

ARMENIA

ANATOLIA

CASPIAN S

TAURUS MOUNTAINS

AMANUS MTS.

Tigris R.

Halaf

Brak

Tepe Gawra

Nineveh

Erbil

Aleppo

Nimrud

Karim Shahir

Alalakh

Hassuna

Jarmo

Assur

Little Zab R.

Great

ZAGROS MOUNTAINS

CYPRUS

Euphrates R.

Mari

Samarra

MEDITERRANEAN SEA

AKKAD

Tell Asmar

Hit

Khafaje

Tell Agrab

Aqar Quf

Jemdet Nasr

SYRIAN DESERT

Kish

Nippur

ELAM

Susa

Lagash

PALESTINE

Jericho

SUMER

Haji Muhammad

Uruk

Jerusalem

DEAD SEA

Larsa

al'Ubaid

Ur

SINAI

Eridu

ARABIAN DESERT

RED SEA

PERSIAN GULF

Hissar

sepolis

Bakun

WHERE IT HAPPENED

Mesopotamia in southwest Asia is today as it was thousands of years ago. The land is rainless, hot and arid. It stretches east and west from the valley watered by two rivers—the Euphrates, 1700 miles long, and the Tigris, 1200 miles long.

Deserts lie to the west of the valley and mountain slopes of Iran to the east. To the north are hills. Along the lower stretches of the rivers, marshland and plain spread southward across the delta to the Persian Gulf. About 10,000 square miles of what was ancient Mesopotamia are today in the Republic of Iraq.

EARLIEST FARMING COMMUNITIES

9000 B.C.   At Karim Shahir in the foothills of the Zagros Mountains, a people harvest wild wheat and barley, domesticate dog and sheep. They develop from food gatherers to food producers.

7000 B.C.   At Jarmo in the Zagros foothills people build mud houses, grow wheat from seed, and herd goats, sheep and pigs. Fifteen levels of human occupation—the lowest ten inhabited by people who did not yet know how to bake clay pots.

PRE-SUMERIANS

5000 B.C.   Farmers begin to migrate southward and settle in the fertile river valley regions.

5000 B.C.   At Hassuna: Beginnings of irrigation, fine pottery, permanent dwellings.

3500 B.C.   At Tell Halaf: Culture spreads over Mesopotamia and trade develops from the Persian Gulf to the Mediterranean.
At Tell al-Ubaid: Mud-brick villages, basic temple form.
Semitic nomads from Syria and the Arabian peninsula invade southern Mesopotamia and intermingle with the Ubaidian people.

SUMERIANS, CITIES

3500 B.C.   Sumerians appear on the banks of the Euphrates River, probably having migrated from Central Asia through Iran.

3500 B.C.   Uruk people, users of metal

2750 B.C.   Hereditary kingship, dynasties begin

2500 B.C.   Akkad cities develop into powerful city-states; temples to ziggurats.

Different cultures overlapped one another. One period did not necessarily end when another began. Hassuna, Halaf, Ubaid are names of cultures, but who the peoples were remains a mystery not yet completely unraveled.

Vase, Khafaje, about 3200 B.C.

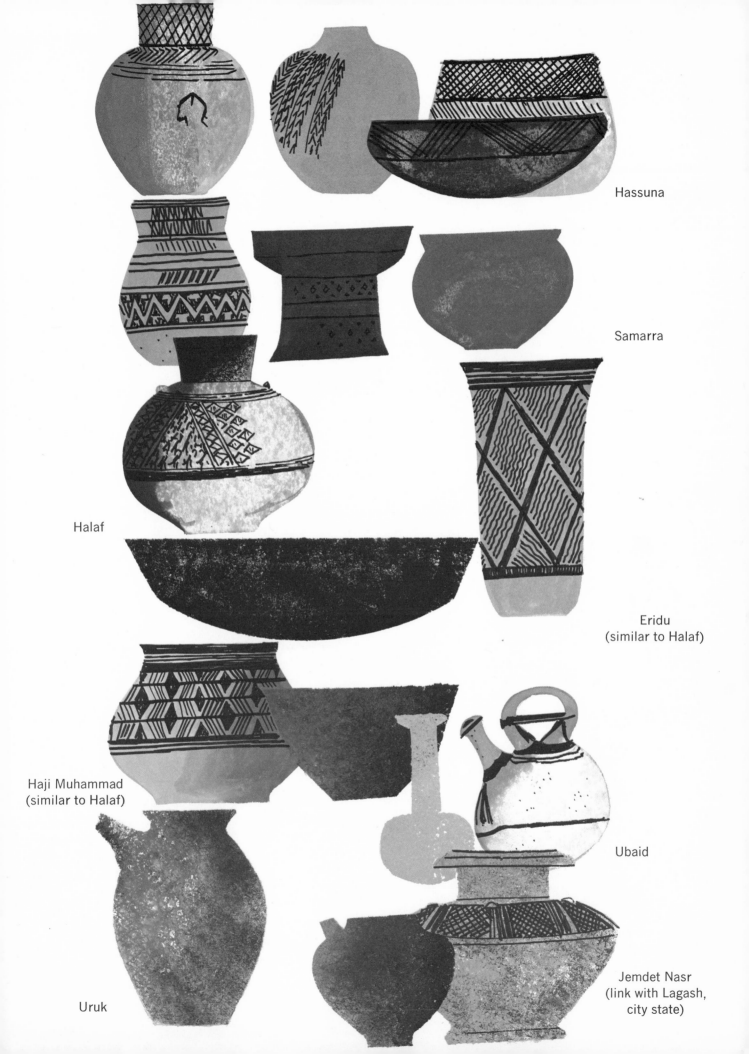

Hassuna

Samarra

Halaf

Eridu
(similar to Halaf)

Haji Muhammad
(similar to Halaf)

Ubaid

Uruk

Jemdet Nasr
(link with Lagash,
city state)

16   Clay map with cuneiform writing
      showing fields and irrigation system
      near Nippur, about 3200 years ago.

IRRIGATION AND FARMING

Mesopotamian marshlands and the river plain were
fertile. The soil was rich. Each year the rivers flooded,
and receding flood waters left muddy sediments along
their channels. Those floods could be dangerous and
destructive too. They often came without warning.
The hot sun baked the land hard and dry during
long seasons without rain. Man needed those river
waters to make farming possible. He must learn to
curb and control the turbulent Tigris and Euphrates.
Banks or levees built up by the Euphrates actually
helped to control its flood waters. But man had to
drain the marshlands and irrigate the rich soil left
behind by the river. Trenches, ditches, and simple
canals were the first necessary steps.

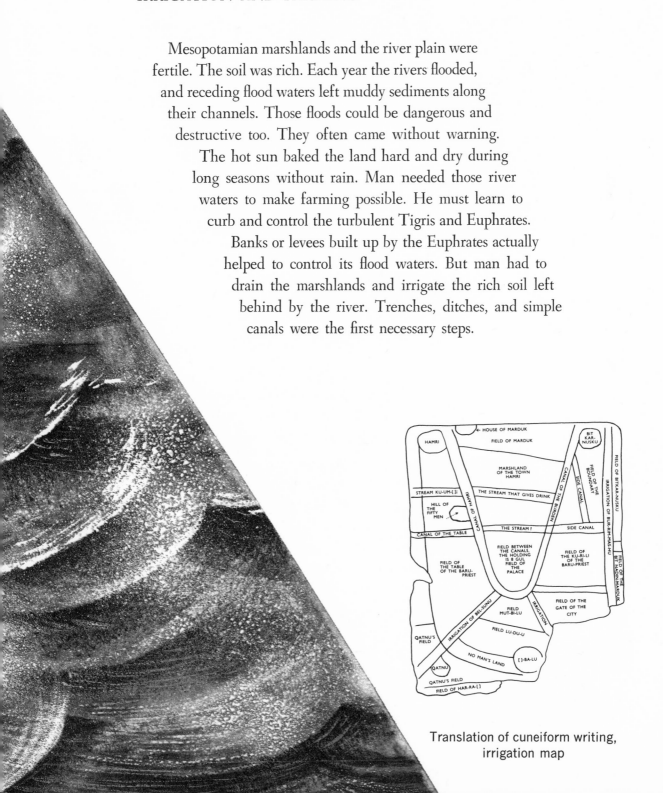

Translation of cuneiform writing,
irrigation map

17

Even the earliest settlers in the valley were using simple forms of drainage and irrigation. But a small group of farmers could never control the river and make it work for growing communities. Only irrigation on a very large scale would assure and protect the crops the rich lands could produce. The efforts of many farmers working together, carefully planned and organized, made farming flourish.

Now man could produce food in great abundance. With irrigation, crops could be grown again and again in the same fields. Irrigation kept the soil nourished. Farmers reaped two harvests a year. More and more land could be cultivated.

With food plentiful, populations grew bigger too in these prehistoric times. Farmers produced abundant crops of barley, emmer and millet. These were the staple grain crops.

Farmers planted vegetable gardens along irrigation canals. They grew many kinds of vegetables—chickpeas, lentils, beans, onions, garlic, leeks, cucumbers, radishes, beets, lettuce, squash, herbs for flavoring, and especially sesame. Sesame oil was burned in temples. Its fragrance was a pleasing part of temple ceremony.

Flax was a most important crop. It supplied the raw material which skilled craftsmen wove into fine cloth. This could be traded for much needed materials not found in the valley.

Fruit trees shaded the vegetable gardens—lemon, quince, pomegranate, fig, apricot, and mulberry. And the fruit trees grew in the shade of the date palms.

Shaduf, a device for lifting water. A long pole mounted on a pillar of wood or rushes daubed with mud is weighted with a clay lump at one end. A bucket is hung from the other. A man operates the shaduf like a seesaw, dipping the bucket into canal or river water.

Three men operating a double lift. The shadufs on mud uprights stand at two levels on the riverbank. In front of each, a brick platform is built out into the river for the men who fill and empty the buckets.

Farmers praised the date palm tree and its 360 uses. From its trunk, boats, doors, wagons and carts could be made. Soaring palm tree trunks formed columns for building lofty temples. From palm ribs, chairs and beds were made. Palm leaves bound together made brooms. The fibers were woven into baskets, rope and fishnets. Young shoots growing at the top of the tree made a tasty salad.

The date itself made a nourishing meal for the poor. It could also be made into honey, vinegar, and wine. Date pits were dried and burned like charcoal, pounded to make flour, or ground and mixed with fodder for cattle in very arid regions.

Supplementing what the fields, gardens and trees provided were steady supplies of meat, fish and fowl. Hunters brought deer, wild boar and gazelles to the people of the city. Fowlers with nets caught birds. Fishermen with net, trap and line brought in many kinds of fish.

Early shaduf, from cylinder seal
3000-2000 B. C.

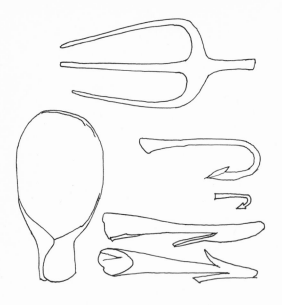

Tools: hoe, fish trident, fishhooks

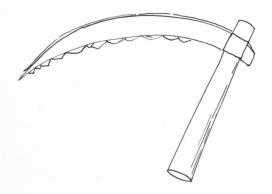

Flint sickle, Hassuna

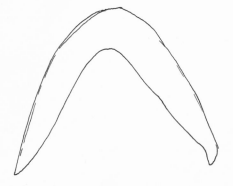

Clay sickle, al'Ubaid

Methods of tilling the greatly increased farm areas had to be improved.

The primitive way of sowing was to drop seeds into holes made with a pointed stick. This was replaced by planting long rows or furrows made with a stone or metal hoe. Al'Ubaidian farmers used heavy flint hoes, which they brought with them into this stoneless land. But even with such a tool they were able to work only very limited areas in the Euphrates valley.

Nobody can tell how long it took or who did it, but over the centuries old tools were improved and new ones invented.

The pickax was used day in, day out, all through the year. With it the farmer dug holes and trenches for irrigation, and built dams to hold back the water. He used it for building shelters for his cattle and sheep.

A farmer who could cultivate a small plot with a flint hoe needed and invented the wooden plow for cultivating his larger fields. First, the land was cultivated by a man with the plow. Later, with less effort, by an ox and a plow.

The pickax and the plow were so important to the farmer that they inspired legends and myths. They were believed to be gifts from a god to his people.

Bigger harvests made it necessary to improve methods of reaping. Sickles of clay fired hard by intense heat had a sharp cutting-edge. This tool the al'Ubaidians found so brittle that it broke easily. But it was simple to make new ones. There was always plenty of clay.

Later the Uruk people coming into Mesopotamia were already using metal. They may have brought copper or bronze sickles with them.

Limestone trough, length 39 inches, Uruk

Bas-relief, a herd of cows and dairying activities. Limestone and shell figures set in black

Butter is being churned, prepared and stored.

Plowing scene, reconstructed from
cylinder seal impression on tablet, Nippur

Marsh reeds growing wild and plentiful were used for basketry, building, furniture and fuel for fire. Reed matting strengthened irrigation dikes.

Farmers were skilled dairymen too. Their bulls, cows and calves provided meat and skin as well as milk and its products. The most useful animal was the ox. He pulled the farmer's plow and also dragged and carried loads.

Flocks of sheep and lambs were raised for wool. They produced the thickest, finest fleece in this ancient world. Farmers kept herds of goats too.

bitumen, framed in copper, from temple of Ninhursag at al'Ubaid, about 2500 B.C.

Cow being milked from rear

Woven goat hair made carpeting and sometimes large containers. The fat and skin of pigs were used as well as the meat. Special swineherds butchered and prepared the meat.

Hides of all these animals were tanned and made into leather goods both for the city dweller and for export.

A fragrant beverage for citizens and gods alike was beer. The goddess in charge of preparing it was Ninkasi, whose name means "the lady who fills the mouth."

Seed plow from stele

23

Exposed foundations of house, Jarmo
Mud walls were built above the stones.

THE CITY—A PLACE

Irrigation in the Euphrates valley made the settled prosperous community possible. As the population grew larger, the place the people built and lived and worked in grew larger too. *villag*

The community was first very small—a hamlet. The growing hamlet became a town, then a small city. A small city grew large. Centuries later, cities became great and powerful—Sumerian city-states. The ruins of these were what archaeologists found below the glories of ancient Babylon they had dug to find.

Archaeologists digging down to unearth an ancient city would find it built upon a man-made mound. Once a side of the city had faced the river. Sometimes a canal might have been made to run through the city.

Thick mud-brick walls protected the town or city from being flooded or washed away. The walls on the

Reconstruction of farmhouse
Hassuna, about 5000 B.C.

waterfront side were a step toward making a protected harbor.

Over the centuries the Euphrates has shifted its course many times. Both the size and shape of the delta pushed out into the Persian Gulf have changed. Because of the changing river course, towns and cities once along its shores are now many miles away from it, surrounded by drifting sands. Today the remains of the great city of Ur, once a seaport, are more than 150 miles inland.

City walls served many purposes. Sometimes for protection—they kept marauders and animals out. Lions and other wild creatures prowled the plains and marshes. Sometimes for pride—they gave the community a sense of importance. A wall gave the whole community a feeling of security against the vast outside world. A city gate was the only point at which anyone could enter or leave.

Clay brick wall, Uruk

Baked clay round house, architectural model
Mari, 2900-2460 B.C.

Erbil today, built on mound over many layers of ancient habitation

Rising higher than any other building within the walls was the temple, for the city belonged to a god. As the community grew larger, the temples grew larger too and spread out over larger areas. And always the sacred building rose higher and higher. Around it grew the sacred area or temenos. Sometimes an outer town grew up beyond the walls. Farmlands stretched farther and farther.

From earliest times there were streets and alleys with houses packed in along them side by side. Refuse of all sorts was thrown from the houses into the street. Streets were narrow and twisty, and remained that way in the older parts of even much later and grander, more prosperous cities.

Houses were built of mud brick. Poorer ones were one story high. Wealthier citizens lived in two-story houses, whitewashed and plastered both outside and in. Houses of poor and rich were jumbled together haphazardly.

Rooms of the house were built around an inner court. Flat roofs were cool and comfortable for sleeping after the sun went down. Thick walls and small openings made these houses suitable for life in a hot, dry, dusty, windy city.

Clay map, city of Nippur about 1500 B.C. Sumerian and Akkadian writing gives names of buildings, rivers and gates. Double lines show main canal dividing city. Euphrates River on far left, temple precinct at far right.

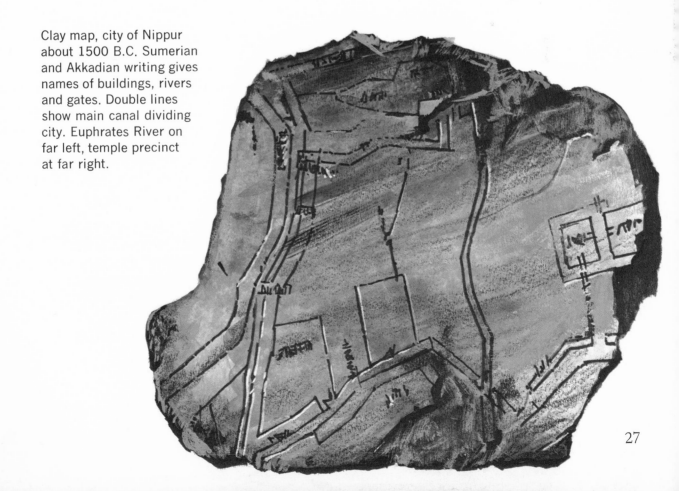

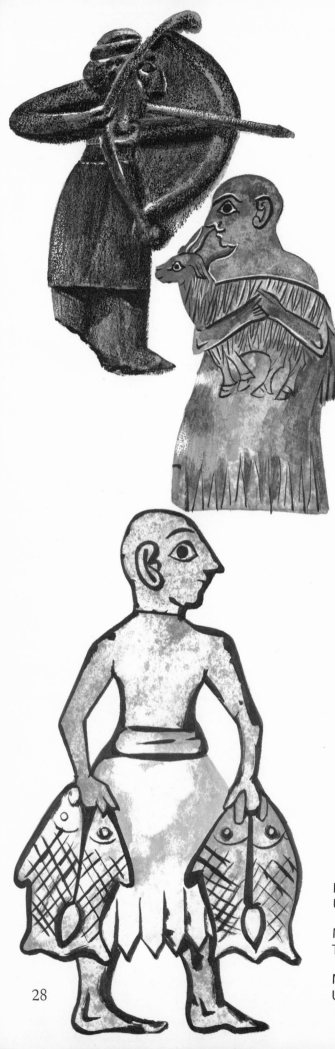

THE CITY—ITS PEOPLE

A city is people. Without people there would be no cities. When you talk about a city, you talk not only about the place but more important about the people who built and lived in that place.

From hamlet, to village, to the earliest city, the community was agricultural, and for centuries the growth of cities depended upon agriculture. Without an abundance of food and the agricultural surplus the farmer produced, there could be no cities.

The earliest flourishing cities had roots far in the past among many peoples. In southern Mesopotamia there was a mingling, an overlapping, of cultures and people. Some of them are known to have migrated into the region. Some were descended from ancestors who had lived there over generations.

Evidence of the times and peoples before written records had been set down is an incomplete and often puzzling picture of what happened. Some parts of that picture are surprisingly vivid and clear. Others still remain a blank—a challenge to archaeologists.

Hunter, stone lion-hunt stele
Uruk, about 2000 B.C.

Man with goat, mother-of-pearl
Temple of Ninhursag at Mari

Man carrying strings of fish
Ur, 4500 years ago

28

The earliest people coming south from the Zagros mountain regions brought with them their clay pots and precious seeds. Over the centuries they flourished and their numbers multiplied. As early communities prospered, Semitic peoples began coming into the valley. Sometimes they came peacefully to share, and sometimes as conquerors to overcome and dominate.

The Mesopotamian culture of these mixed peoples spread from the Mediterranean to the Caspian Sea. Probably there was even an exchange between the river peoples of Mesopotamia and those along the Nile in Egypt and the Indus in India.

Last to migrate into the region were the Sumerians, probably from central Asia by way of Iran. They adopted and built upon the developed culture they found already there. Sumerian historians write of their own beginnings as if they had been there since the creation of the world.

In the earliest hamlet, basic loyalty was still to the family. Farming was a family activity. As food became more abundant, the size of families increased.

Warrior, shell inlay, height 4⅜ inches
Mari, 2900-2460 B.C.

Prisoner, shell inlay, height 3⅞ inches
Mari, 2900-2460 B.C.

Armed warrior, shell inlay, height 3⅞ inches
Mari, 2900-2460 B.C.

The hamlet was now a group of farming families, and loyalties shifted to the group. This gave a sense of unity. Without this unity the community could never have engaged in irrigation on a very large scale.

Without unity the people would never have acted together to work out an organization, never have accepted the rules and regulation necessary for growth. The early community was a cooperative venture. It was the duty of every citizen to contribute to its support as well as share in the benefits of living together in a community.

The people of the city were united even more by their acceptance and belief in a single god. Each city thought of itself as the people of one god among the family of gods. He was patron deity of all of them. He protected them. He saw to their well-being.

In return, man was servant of his god. He devoted much energy to filling the temple granaries and warehouses. For his god he built the temple always more spacious and soaring.

The surplus produced by the farmer and stored in the temple made the community prosperous. The effort of the whole community was no longer needed to make sure they all had enough to eat.

Now not everybody was needed to farm. Some could become craftsmen. There was a demand for what they made, not only at the temple but among the people of the city, and of other, smaller com-

Alabaster statue, Ebih-il temple steward
height 20⅝ inches, about 2500 B.C.

Gypsum figure, worshiper, height 17¾ inches
Temple of Ishtar at Mari, about 2500 B.C.

munities. Sometimes the craftsmen's wares were exported to far distant places.

With the surplus it became necessary to keep records. A tally was kept of produce devoted to the temple and stored there. Records of the exchange of goods must be kept. The temple came to be the place where much business was carried on.

The production and storage of grain—wealth—irrigation, specialization and exchange of products, the very increase in population made leadership and more formal rules and laws governing all these matters necessary.

At first villages and towns were democratic. They were governed by two groups. The General Assembly was made up of free citizens. A Council of Elders also were free men selected by the citizens to act for them.

The Council of Elders, the temple priests and other officials were usually chosen from rich and powerful families. As wealth increased, all citizens were no longer on an equal basis.

At times the community faced crises. The river might flood over it, irrigation might break down. The town might be under attack. At such moments all citizens banded together to cope with the emergency. In case of attack the Assembly and its Council would choose a strong leader to head the defense of the city. His power was temporary and ended when the crisis was over.

A   Marble statue, woman wearing cloak
     height 9 inches, 2900-2460 B.C.

B   Alabaster statue of woman with headdress
     typical of Mari, height about 9 inches
     Temple of Ishtar at Mari, 2900-2460 B.C.

C   Head of woman, Tell Agrab

D   Woman with turban, Tell Agrab

E   Figure of woman, height about 8 inches, Khafaje

As villages and towns grew richer, more often subject to attack, a permanent strong leadership was needed. The Council chose a "big man" or king, known as a lugal. He was god's representative on earth, just as the people were god's children.

By far the greatest number of people were those who produced—farmers, fishermen, hunters, builders of all sorts and the craftsmen—all free men. Tradesmen were a most important part of this group.

The least fortunate group were the slaves. A man might become a slave for many different reasons, in many different ways. Prisoners captured in battle often became slaves, but could be ransomed. Slaves might be purchased abroad. A bankrupt father might sell himself and his family into slavery, but for no more than three years.

A slave had definite legal rights. He could own property, engage in business and eventually buy his freedom.

Limestone figure of woman
height 11¾ inches, 2900-2460 B.C.

Some of the wealthiest and most powerful people centered in the temple. They administered its growing wealth and power. They were served by a very large group of craftsmen, workmen, servants of all kinds, including many slaves.

Before there was writing, the city had produced a varied culture, with peoples engaged in many and varied activities. It had amassed wealth and grown from a hamlet to a group of about two thousand.

Stone figure of scribe, inscription on back difficult to interpret, probably dedicated to god Ningirsu by a man called A-im-dugud for the life of the scribe Dudu, height 15⅜ inches, 2900-2460 B.C.

ARCHITECTURE

Reed hut building, basic structure

Cities of the plain rose up in ancient Mesopotamia from mud to monumental shrines, and returned in time to rubble and mounds of drifting sand.

The Euphrates River plain and delta provided endless mud, many reeds and some palm trees. The first builders used whatever material was close at hand. Houses were made of reeds plastered with mud and supported on reed platforms.

Material determined the form of building. First, bundles of tall reeds bound together were planted in the ground. Single stems were not strong enough to resist wind. Smaller bundles were lashed to the uprights as crossbars and formed a framework.

Marsh Arab reed house
southern Iraq today

Remains of similar reed houses
have been found at Ur.

Reed matting fastened to the framework made walls. Additional uprights lengthened the walls and made a more tunnel-like room. Sides and roof were plastered with mud. Fresh mud coating added from time to time made the walls very thick.

Bending the tops of the reeds from the corners inward and tying them together at the center created a dome. The long tunnel-shaped room with its reed and mud-covered roof produced the arch and vault.

The maker of reed houses gained experience and knowledge of building principles. The city builder adapted these techniques of marshland building to mud-brick architecture.

In time builders discovered that reeds were not essential to building, especially when buildings needed to be made larger. Hardened mud itself might serve better than reeds. Basketfuls of stiff kneaded clay piled load upon load were used first to make garden walls. Then some builder realized that small lumps of clay held together by mud mortar would build an even better wall.

Bricks at first were clay lumps pressed together by hand. Later they were molded in an open wooden rectangular frame. Chopped straw or dung mixed with clay prevented warping and cracking. The oldest known examples of bricks, found side by side with reed hut building, come from al'Ubaid times.

Sometimes the bricks were hand-shaped and hardened by the sun. Sometimes they were baked in a kiln. Burnt bricks were used at first only for important buildings and mostly in the foundations. As the country grew richer, kiln-fired bricks were more lavishly used.

Within the thick-walled area of the city, houses were one- or two-story, mud-brick buildings. They were flat-roofed, with no windows and a low door. Rooms were grouped around an open court. Walls sometimes six feet thick kept the house cool in spite of the fierce heat and glare of the sun.

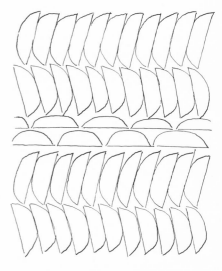

Brick walls, set in one kind of "herringbone" pattern 3000-2000 B.C.

Bricks with cuneiform stamping

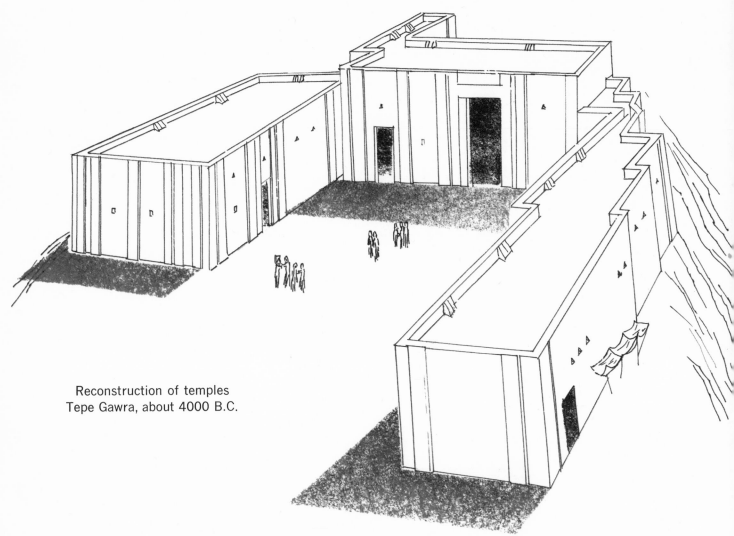

Reconstruction of temples
Tepe Gawra, about 4000 B.C.

The largest, tallest, most important building in the city was the temple, God's house. It was built on a high terrace of mud brick. Using patterns suggested by reed buildings, temple architects achieved a feeling of height and grandeur.

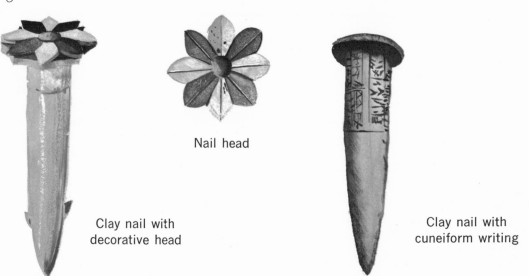

Nail head

Clay nail with
decorative head

Clay nail with
cuneiform writing

The building usually consisted of a rectangular shrine room or cella. In the cella was a niche for the god's statue. An offering table made of mud brick stood before it. As the temple grew, the cella was surrounded by rooms used for temple activities.

Pillars became a part of the grander, larger temple structure. The earliest columns yet found were part of a temple at Erech in Mesopotamia. A central core of palm wood supported mud bricks, making full-round and half-round columns.

Baked clay cones, shaped somewhat like sticks of chalk and painted various colors, were driven into the soft clay of columns and walls. The colored heads of these cones made geometric patterns—a mosaic. Sometimes the mosaic resembled the pattern of the palm tree bark itself and added interest to surfaces. At excavation sites in Erech, hundreds of these clay cones can still be found.

Today throughout the marshlands, Arabs still build houses of reed and mud exactly as ancient Mesopotamians built. The Mesopotamian reed and mud house, the oldest architectural style in history, has continued over centuries to inspire the use and development of mosaic, columns, arches, vaulted roofs and buttresses.

Cone mosaics from Eanna temple precinct, Uruk, about 3500 B.C.

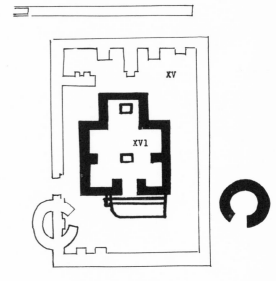

Plan of temples, Eridu levels XV, XVI, about 4200 B.C.

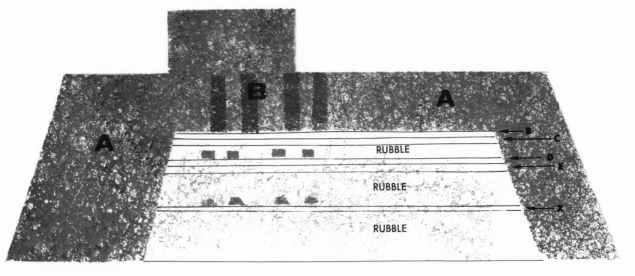

Diagrammatic section through tell at Uruk. Lowest level X is supposed foundation of first temple built on this site. Levels D and E indicate foundations of two later temples. C shows still more recent temple platform. At B, ruins of White Temple and walls, later encased in brickwork A.

Warka vase, alabaster, decoration
in relief representing offering scene,
Uruk, shrine of goddess Inanna
about 3200-3100 B.C., perhaps earlier

ARTS

From the most ancient times art has been very close to religion.

The earliest settlers brought decorated pots and some religious figures with them into the Euphrates valley. They were already involved with art forms.

Man's sacred duty was first to build a house for his god. It was in the architectural arts that these people excelled. Of painting very little remains. Ruined clay walls still show some evidence of painted murals, sometimes even large areas of color. Almost nothing has been found of recognizable figures or designs. These have not survived the effects of time and the destructive forces of both nature and man.

An altar, an offering table, statues, and cult objects had to be placed in the temple so that man could communicate with his god. From hand-modeled clay figures to painted vessels, the first craftsmen worked to supply these needs. As the temples grew more awesome and dramatic, temple accessories became richer and richer.

Despite limited materials, these craftsmen developed unique techniques and skills. Clay and clay and more clay was the only material at hand. Stone, wood, metal and all other materials must be obtained by trade—often in exchange for objects the artisan had manufactured.

Within the sacred precinct of the temple man placed statues of the god and of himself. Life for the busy citizen was full and much too short. Believing that prayer and faithful temple attendance would assure his well-being and a longer life, a man would have a portrait statue made of himself. As if by magic this sculpted form was endowed with a life of its own. It would stand forever before his god's statue to express absentee devotion.

In Mesopotamia stone was hard to obtain. Large stone slabs from other regions were expensive and difficult to bring into this stoneless plain. Stonecutters had to make do with small pieces. In spite of this handicap, the skill and imagination of stonecutters contributed much to the arts. They developed relief carving on plaques and steles, on commemorative pieces, bowls and vases, showing us with carved flat forms how their people lived.

The Mesopotamian stonecutter created the cylinder seal. The seal was a small stone cylinder with a hole through its center. A cord or metal pin could be inserted and the seal could be worn by its owner. Its surface was covered with figures of animals, barns, boats, gods and people. The seal had a very practical use, but it became an art form. Today it provides an invaluable record. In spite of the scarcity of stone, more stone pieces have survived over the centuries. Things fashioned of the more destructible clay have been damaged and lost.

A carved stone seal rolled over a soft clay tablet, the clay cover of a jar, or a bit of clay attached to any kind of storage container was the sign of ownership.

The carvings of animals on seals or reliefs of any kind were almost without equal in that ancient world. Because animals were an important part of an agricultural community's life, it was natural for sculptors to depict them tenderly and realistically. Sculptors endowed them with a feeling of the fullness of life.

Perhaps because material was scarce, craftsmen exploited fully whatever came their way. The art of inlay developed, to add colorful interest to surfaces and objects. Bits of shell, stone, or ivory were set in bitumen. Carpenters reused wood not only for furniture but for boats, wagons, and chariots.

The arts of the earliest Mesopotamian people were limited beginnings of shapes and forms that others coming after them would adapt and develop on a far grander scale.

Head of woman, white marble, eyes and eyebrows originally inlaid, height 7⅞ inches Uruk, 2800-2600 B.C.

Votive tablet, slate, hole for fastening to wall, height 7½ inches, Nippur

Cylinder seal and imprint horned antelope with vegetation about 3200 B.C.

Stone bowl, reliefs of bulls and ears of corn
height 2⅛ inches, Ur, about 3200 B.C.

Boar's head, glazed pottery,
used as wall ornament

Limestone bull
height 8½ inches, about 3200 B.C.

Bull, bronze plating on wood,
Temple at al'Ubaid,
height 47 inches, about 3500 B.C.

Wolf's head, gold and silver alloy (electrum),
gold wire teeth, ears and jaws attached
by pins, head and eye sockets filled with
bitumen, Tepe Gawra, about 3200 B.C.

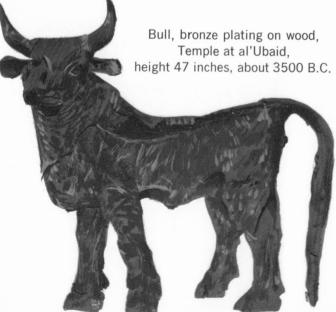

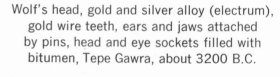

Clay sheep's head, height 3¾ inches

Copper relief, lion-headed eagle god Im-dugud with two stags
Temple of Ninhursag, al'Ubaid, height 42 inches, length about 92 inches
Reconstructed from thousands of fragments

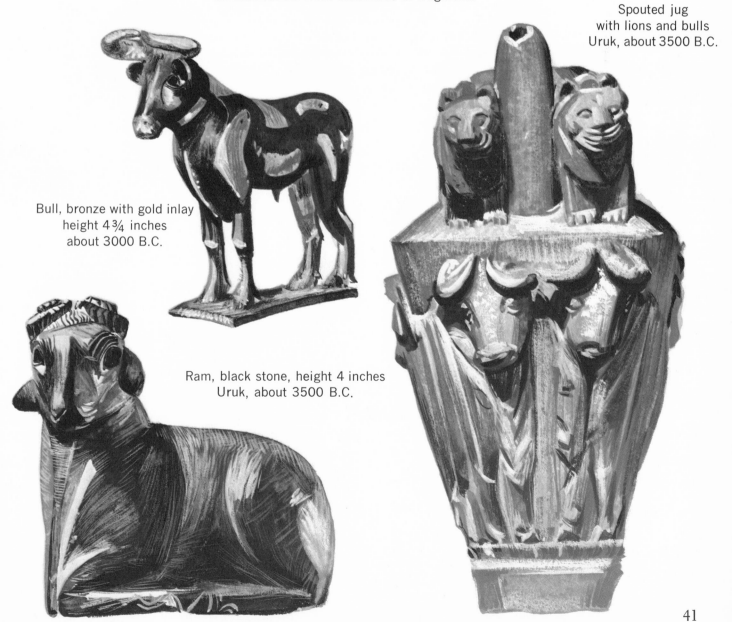

Spouted jug
with lions and bulls
Uruk, about 3500 B.C.

Bull, bronze with gold inlay
height 4¾ inches
about 3000 B.C.

Ram, black stone, height 4 inches
Uruk, about 3500 B.C.

RELIGION

Religion was at the very heart of the life of Mesopotamian communities. Had not the gods created the earth and man and made them both fertile? Was not man the servant of the gods?

The earliest immigrants coming into Mesopotamia brought their religious beliefs with them. Each family or clan brought its particular deity.

As loyalty shifted from family or clan to the community, the whole group became the people of one protective god. Other communities had other gods. But the gods themselves were all one large family. Throughout this ancient land there was a common belief in the same gods. And each god had divine powers. His word could create something out of nothingness. His power could keep his people safe and secure.

When temples were small and intimate, god's people felt they could communicate directly with him. As temples grew large and powerful and temple affairs more complicated, a group of temple priests acted as god's representatives.

Female figure, Ur, and
male figure, Eridu, terra-cotta
height 5½ inches, about 3500 B.C.

God, Anu, seal impression
height 2½ inches, Mari, about 3000 B.C.

Votive plaque, representation of god
Khafaje, 2900-2460 B.C.

The gods created the world and all that exists and all that moves in it. When the gods spoke their words must be obeyed. But they were human too, doing what humans do and looking much like them. Man saw himself as the clay of the earth, molded by the gods to serve the gods.

Greatest of all were the supreme deities in control of the universe. God of heaven was An and his city was Erech. Enlil, the air god, was the guardian of the city of Nippur. Enki was the water god and his city was Eridu. And Ninhursag was the mother earth goddess, the mother of all living things.

Less powerful than the supreme gods but superior to men were the demons. Good demons protected temples, houses and humans. Wicked demons were believed to be restless spirits of the dead who lived in tombs, in darkness and in the desert. They brought terror and torment to the earth.

As cities grew, so did temples and all the temple properties. Not unlike a complicated big business, temples required large storerooms and rooms in which to carry on the exchange of goods. Male and female priests had different jobs to perform. Ceremonies, rites and rituals required anointers, chanters, sacrificers, wailers, sorcerers, magicians and diviners.

The temple staff included bakers, brewers, butchers, shepherds, boatmen, musicians and dancers, as well as the large staff even small temples required.

Sun god Utu, about 2500 B.C.

Enki, god of water and wisdom,
with his two-faced minister
Isimud, about 2200 B.C.

Goddess Ninhursag, vase fragment,
height 9⅞ inches, about 2200 B.C.

Nintu, goddess of births
terra-cotta, height 4 inches

Terra-cotta demon,
Humbaba, height 4 inches   43

Quffa, circular tublike boat
built of skin-covered reeds and
propelled by elaborate oars

TRADE, RIVER AND LAND TRANSPORT

Trade more than anything else brought prosperity to the Mesopotamian cities.

With little wood, stone or minerals, but with larger amounts of surplus grain, even the earliest farmers in ancient Mesopotamia had to trade for what they needed. And trading took them to far places.

The swift-running Tigris and the meandering Euphrates made river transport easy and economical. Strong currents brought vessels easily and rapidly downstream. There was little use for oars, paddles or poles except to keep the craft midstream. Traffic on the waters was one way. No headway could be made north against the flow.

Still plying the same waters today as they did in ancient times are three different types of river craft.

In northern Mesopotamia, where there was timber, wooden boats were built. Some were as much as thirty feet long. The stern was square and the bow

Cylinder seal impression
reed boat, Eanna temple precinct
Uruk, about 3500 B.C.

Silver boat, tomb at Ur, about 2400 B.C.

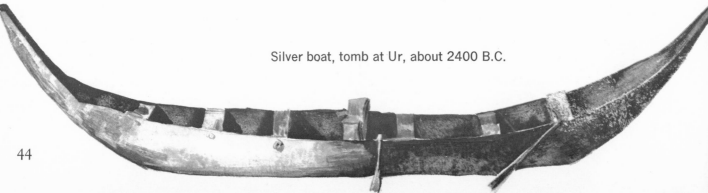

blunt. The sides were covered with almost straight heavy planking. This boat used a triangular sail.

Another vessel, the coracle, is today called the quffa. This boat, in ancient times called the turnip, was shaped like a tub. It was made of reeds, covered with skin and coated with bitumen for waterproofing.

A third craft was a raft of timbers lashed together and buoyed up by inflated skins. This was called a kalakku, today known as a kelek. Even animals and blocks of stone could be carried on this raft.

When boats reached their destination many were dismantled. The leather covering of the quffa was stripped from the wicker frame and placed on donkey-back to be returned north and reused for another downstream voyage. The kelek was dismantled and the logs were either reused or sold for timber.

Cargos coming down the Tigris included timber, copper, and obsidian, a volcanic glass. From Hit on the Euphrates came bitumen, a heavy petroleum product used for waterproofing and as a kind of cement. At this ancient site the production of bitu-men, one of the oldest industries in the world, is still carried on. Cedar wood from the Amanus Moun-tains, a branch of the Taurus range, was first dragged by men and oxen from Alalakh via Aleppo. Then it was carried to the river at a point where it runs nearest to the Mediterranean.

Quffa on Tigris today

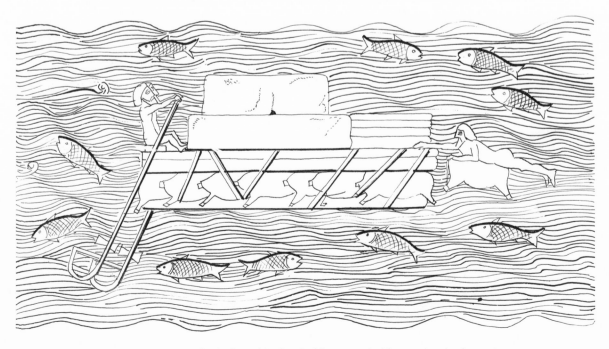

Kelek, raft supported by inflated animal skins, carried heavy loads downstream.

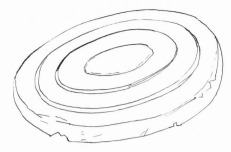

Clay potter's wheel, Uruk, about 2000 B.C.

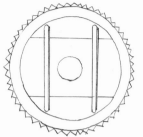

Wheel, nail-studded
Susa, about 2500 B.C.

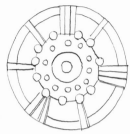

Wheel with copper tire
Susa

Men carrying vessel on pole

Man carrying load
supported by thongs
of headband over forehead

All raw materials so necessary to the arts and crafts had to be brought into the cities in return for agricultural produce or manufactured articles. It was in copper, brought from the far northern hills of Armenia and from Elam to the east, that the earliest smiths worked. They gained a profitable livelihood and a reputation for skilled craftsmanship.

Craftsmen themselves sometimes came from foreign parts to work for temples in Mesopotamian cities. Soon these workers became the most skilled artisans in the ancient world. Chisel workers sculpted figurines of ivory and wood. Jewelers worked in gold and silver and used imported stones such as lapis lazuli, carnelian and topaz.

Most important in the development of commerce and trade was the textile industry. Thousands of tons of fine wool and flax produced some of the finest cloth in the ancient world. Linen garments were used by temple priests and holy men.

The invention of the wheel in Mesopotamia transformed the pottery industry and about the same time revolutionized transport. Clay models, toys or votive objects are evidence that wheeled vehicles were used in the early cities.

On land, supplies, manufactured items and farm produce were transported by man and beast—with sledges and wagons. Because of the wheel, land travel was becoming more possible, but the real trade routes and lifelines remained the waterways.

46

Chariot with pegged wooden wheels
Ur, about 2500 B.C.

Pictographs, cart and sledge
Uruk, about 3500 B.C.

Votive wheeled chariot
about 3500 B.C.

Vase of Entemena, a priest-king of Lagash, silver mounted on brass pedestal,
engraved lion-headed eagle with lions, stags and border of heifers,
height 13¾ inches, about 2500 B.C. This piece was found unbroken.

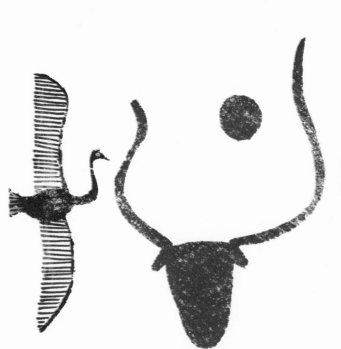

Patterns, Halaf ware

Ubaid style dish, Ur, about 2500 B.C.

Early picture writing

Pictographs on
clay tablet
Circles represent numbers.

Signs on tablet, Kish, about 3500 B.C.
Head, hand, foot, threshing sledge

48

Earliest pictograph tablets, Uruk

FROM PICTOGRAPHS TO WRITING

The first people roaming the earth in search of food and shelter were deeply involved with sky changes, star positions, moon phases, the sun's movement and the season's change. When man learned to plant seeds and grow and harvest grain, to farm and produce food, then he settled in one place.

Now the change of seasons became even more meaningful to him. Nature itself gave man signs. Suddenly the waters surged, flocks of birds flew overhead, buds swelled, green shoots appeared. Spring was on the way. Now it was time to plant the seed.

Certain things could be expected to happen at the same time each year. Man came to realize that he could plan for these times if he set down a sign or a mark. Just with a line or a simple picture he could begin to keep records. He could give a message. A single picture or a number of pictures put together could tell a story, tell what he had to do or what he had done. He could pass on to someone else what he observed.

Picture symbols became a first step in the development of writing.

In the earliest of cities everyone had to pay a certain amount to the gods—so many sheep or cattle, so much grain, so many jars of butter. Taxation had begun.

Temple priests had to keep records. Payments were made to the temple—so many bushels of barley, so much sesame oil, so many fish. Produce and cloth were also given out in exchange for labor and other services made to the temple.

In the beginning of record keeping, man used a sharpened reed to scratch outlines of pictures into fresh clay. Sheep and cows, milk containers, farm tools, a human head, a bundle of reeds—a symbol of the goddess Inanna. Picture marks on small tablets of clay were used as tags attached to sacks of grain and other products in containers. These tags told what was in the container and its quantity. These line pictures show us a part of early community life.

Heaven, water and earth, god and the stars were signs which had always been deeply significant to man. A great variety of symbols with religious significance had already been used in pottery design.

The sharpened reed used by the painter to decorate pots was also used to make picture records on clay. The pointed end of this stylus made pictographs. As time passed, these pictures became more stylized and simpler to make. Finally there was a series of signs, like a form of script. Hundreds of different signs made it necessary for a scribe to spend years learning to use them correctly.

In time the reed stylus was no longer sharpened. The reed to be used as a stylus was cut straight across. It was blunt and made a wedge-shaped mark. This triangular-shaped end of the reed pressed into wet clay left records and told stories thousands of years before there was a written language. The pictures were not writing, but they were the basis of the writing to come.

Development from pictures to cuneiform signs
Bird, fish, donkey, ox, sun, grain, orchard, plow, boomerang, foot

Pictograph tablet, Uruk, about 3500 B.C.
Probably statement of temple accounts

Clay tag

Shale plaque shaped like chisel
Earliest Near Eastern pictures and writing
combined, about 3500 B.C.

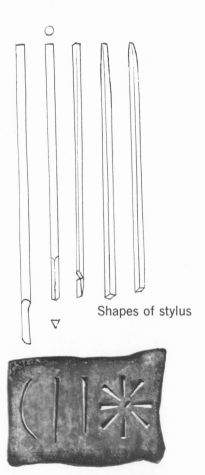

Shapes of stylus

Strokes made by scratching with pointed stylus
Later marks made by pressing triangular stylus
into damp clay. Finally stylus became blunter
and marks more clearly wedge-shaped.

Little by little the pattern of tiny wedge-shaped symbols came to stand for sounds. Now what had begun as pictographs was becoming a written language. The marks made up a system of cuneiform writing—cuneiform means wedge-shaped.

As far back as man had lived he used speech—at first, probably very few simple sounds for simple communication. Speaking is really an exchange of sounds. Now that a sign made in clay stood for a sound, it created a problem. The same sound often had several meanings. Only its use could make clear which meaning was the intended one.

In the same way a simple symbol had several meanings. This is the reason why archaeological scholars spent endless time studying and comparing countless records before they could understand the language. The written records lasted and had been found. But there was no one to tell what the man who left the record was saying.

Since symbols represented sounds, it was easy for the later Babylonians and Assyrians to pick up and use the system of symbols which had been slowly developing over many hundreds of years before them.

Archaeologists digging from the surface down came first on the remains of these later civilizations. As they went farther and farther down and back in time, they found earlier symbols, some of which did not represent sounds. They were going backward in the history of writing as well as of people. In that way they discovered the earliest records in the pictures which preceded writing.

Once cuneiform writing was deciphered, they were able to read records on tablets, on memorial plaques, on a great variety of objects. Now they could know far more and much more exactly about the man and the life of the early farmers who had developed a culture out of which came the large-scale Babylonian and Assyrian cities.

Inscription on rock of Behistun, Persia, about 500 B.C., with bas-relief
life-size figures, Darius the Persian king receiving prisoners. Script, 1306 lines,
provided the key to deciphering cuneiform writing. Inscription was carved in
three languages—Old Persian, Akkadian and Elamite. With this as a key, thousands
of cuneiform tablets from Mesopotamia can now be read.

CONCLUSION

These then were the beginnings, foundations out of which grew the earliest of cities. They set the pattern for Sumer, the earliest civilized city. The pattern for Babylonia and the cities of Assyria which came after—in fact for every modern city anywhere in the world.

It is important to realize that the changes which took place before farming began happened over a very long time—many thousands of years.

From the time of the earliest farming communities, the pace of change quickened. Changes which might have spread out over many thousands of years now crowded into a few hundred. Settled farming communities became flourishing cities in a very brief span of time.

Today the basic elements remain much the same wherever cities may be. A city depends on a source of food, though farming is probably not the basis of its growth and prosperity. Trade and transport, from their beginnings in ancient Mesopotamia, have continued to gain in importance.

There is probably no city wall but there are twisty narrow streets and jumbles of houses rich and poor crowded in together. There are tall buildings and spired churches. Laws and taxation are still necessary. City records must still be kept.

The ancient sky-soaring temples, the great walls, gates and palaces, the people of very mixed blood and their different gods are long since gone. Today all that remains of them lies buried deep under desolate heaps of drifted sand, where once irrigation and river waters made great fields of wheat and barley flourish.

But their world, their ideas, do live on in other ways, even for those unaware of their very name. Archaeologists and other scholars continue to unearth, restore, and reconstruct their remains. For as long as someone uses a wheel, sails a ship, charts a star's position, wears linen, fashions metal, counts with numbers, writes, irrigates to farm, builds with arches, vaults, domes, and columns, we are indebted.

Now the city has grown so vast that as neighboring cities keep stretching farther and farther they may merge into an urban unit of the future—megalopolis.

Minaret of the Friday Mosque near Samarra, built about 1100 years ago

GODS   DEMONS   CITIES

The pre-Sumerian people believed in a religion that was animistic. Man was surrounded by gods and demons, large and powerful forces that shaped his life and being. Each city worshiped a patron god, who protected his people and saw to their well-being.

Man—and gods too—had to be protected from demons, who bore many names and shapes. Man's gods were endowed with superhuman powers, but they also shared very human characteristics.

Here is a list of some of the most important gods and demons.

AN (ANU) was god of heaven and chief god of the pantheon. The Sumerians recognized him as the king of heaven who existed before human kings were on earth. They also believed that earthly kingship was a gift from heaven. His special city was Uruk (Erech).

ENLIL was god of the earth and son of An. His name means "Lord Wind." He was worshiped in all of the cities of Sumer. His particular city was Nippur.

ENKI (EA), the water god and the god of wisdom, was worshipped at Eridu, the oldest of the Sumerian cities, where Sumerian culture emerged.

IMDUGUD, the lion-headed eagle god whose name means "Savage Wind," was known during the time of the great Sumerian kings. He appeared to one of them, Gudea, in a dream, commanding him to rebuild the temple at Babylon.

INNIN (INANNA) (ISHTAR), the goddess of love and fertility, was represented by the planet Venus. She was the principal deity of an important cult at the Eanna Temple of Uruk (Erech).

HUMBABA (HUWAWA) was an ogre, whether god or demon is uncertain, who was warden of the cedar forest. His voice was the hurricane, his mouth the fire god, his breath was death. He was killed by the hero in *The Epic of Gilgamesh*. Gilgamesh was a powerful lugal of Erech during the dynastic period.

NINGIRSU (NINURTA), the warrior god, was god of the storm and the hunt. His temple, E Ninnu, was situated in the city of Lagash.

NINHURSAG (NINTU) (MAMI), goddess of births and mother of all living things, was the wife of Enki.

UTU (SHAMASH), the sun god and the god of justice, was the son of the moon god Sin and brother of Ishtar. He was associated with the cities of Sippar and Larsa.

GLOSSARY AND PRONUNCIATION GUIDE

AKKAD (ä′ käd) — The northern part of Babylonia.

AL′UBAID (al o͞o ba′ ēd) — Culture of great importance and long duration based on a peasant economy extensively using clay for tools and vessels. First unified civilization of Mesopotamia. Probably the earliest form of Sumerian culture.

AN (än) — God of heaven.

ANU (ä′ no͞o) — Same as An above.

BEHISTUN (bā′-his- tün) — Ruined town in western Iran.

EANNA (ā än′ nä) — Great temple of Uruk in which Innin was honored. The temple was so powerful at one time that it was synonymous with Uruk.

ELAM (ē′ lam), Also called Susiana — Ancient kingdom east of Babylonia and north of Persian Gulf.

ELAMITE (ē′ la mit′) — **Language of ancient Elam** spoken as late as the first century B.C. and written in both linear and cuneiform script.

ENKI (en′kē) — God of wisdom.

ENLIL (en lēl′) — National god of Sumer.

ERBIL (ĭr′ bil) — Town in northern Iraq built on site of ancient Arbailu, Assyria.

ERECH (ē′ rek) — Biblical name of Uruk.

ERIDU (ā′ ri do͞o) — Ancient Sumerian city devoted to the worship of Ea (Enki).

HAJI MUHAMMAD (hazh′ i mo͞o ham′ əd) — A culture of south Iranian origin, ancestor of the Ubaid culture, characterized by pottery decorated with glaze paint in dark brown, dark violet, dark green and bright red in geometric patterns.

HALAF (hə läf) — The Neolithic culture unearthed at a mound in Syria was characterized by adobe dwellings and polychrome pottery (red, black and white) decorated with animal designs and geometric patterns.

HASSUNA (has so͞o′ nə) — Excavation site in northern part of Mesopotamia not far from Nineveh which revealed a culture whose pottery ranged from plain coarse cream ware to incised and red painted cream ware.

HUMBABA = HUWAWA (ho͞o va′ va) — Deity or demon of dynastic era in Sumer.

IMDUGUD (im do͞o′ gəd) — A god in animal form.

INANNA (ē nä′ nä) — Sumerian goddess of love and war.

ISHTAR (ish′ tär) — Assyrian and Babylonian goddess of love and war.

JARMO (jär′ mō) — Site of excavations in the foothills of Zagros Mountains.

JEMDET NASR (jem′ dət näz′ ər) — Culture flourished before and led into the Hassuna. Excavated site near the ancient Sumerian city of Kish yielded stone vessels with carved figures and earliest forms of writing.

KARIM SHAHIR (ka rēm′ sha hēr) — Early Neolithic culture of northern Iraq characterized by stone objects such as querns, rings and beads.

KHAFAJE (kä′ fä yā′) — Site of ancient city in eastern Iraq in which remains of walled temple oval were discovered.

KISH (kish) — Ancient Sumerian and Akkadian city about eight miles east of Babylon in southern Iraq.

LAGASH (lā′ gash) — Ancient Sumerian city between Tigris and Euphrates rivers from which were unearthed a palace, statues and clay tablets. Modern village of Telloh, Iraq, is located on the site.

MARI (mä′ rē) — City on the middle Euphrates founded by Semites from Arabia or Syria toward the end of the Jemdet Nasr period. Important source of cuneiform tablets.

MEGALOPOLIS (meg ə lop′ ə lis) — An urban region consisting of several large cities and suburbs that adjoin each other.

NINGIRSU (nin gir′ soo) — God of the Girsu quarter of the city of Lagash.

NINHURSAG (nin hoor′ sag) — Mother earth goddess.

NINTU (nin′ too) — Another form of designation for Ningursu.

NIPPUR (nip poor′) — Ancient Sumerian city in southern Iraq.

SAMARRA (sə mä′ ra) — City on the middle Tigris from which was excavated painted pottery with geometrical designs and stylized animals.

SHADUF (shä doof′) — Irrigation contrivance.

SHAMASH (shä′ mäsh) — Akkadian sun god.

STELE (stē′ lē) — Upright stone pillar bearing an inscription or design and serving as monument.

SUMER (soo′ mər) — Ancient region in southern Mesopotamia where cities were first established. Some of these cities—Ur, Uruk, Kish and Lagash—are major archaeological sites.

SUMERIAN (soo mēr′ eān) — Of or belonging to Sumer, its people and language. World's oldest written documents are Sumerian pictographs and cuneiform tablets.

SUSA (soo′ sä)—Capital of ancient Elam where stele containing the code of Hammurabi was found.

TELL AGRAB (tell a′ grab) — Archaeological site east of Baghdad where both pottery and metal (copper) vessels were found.

TEMENOS (tem′ ə nos) — Sacred enclosure containing a temple and other buildings dedicated to a god.

TEPE GAWRA (te′ pe gou rä′) — Archaeological site in northern Iraq near Mosul.

UR (ûr) — Ancient Sumerian city on the Euphrates where the mighty ziggurat and the royal tombs of the Sumerians were found.

URUK (oo′ rook) — Ancient Sumerian city of tremendous importance and recorded in the Bible as Erech.

UTU (oo′ too) — Sumerian sun god.

WARKA (var′ kə) — Modern site built over the ancient city of Uruk.

ZAGROS (zag′ rəs) — Mountain range in southwest Iran.

ZIGGURAT (zig′ oo rat)′— A temple of Sumerian origin in the form of a pyramidal tower consisting of a number of stories presenting the appearance of a series of terraces.

MEN WHO "DISCOVERED" SUMER AND THE SUMERIANS

The author is indebted to Dr. Samuel Noah Kramer as archaeological adviser and for providing primary and secondary source material, biographical résumés of the key people involved in the beginnings of cities, and especially for "Mr. Sumerian's" knowledge and wit.

HENRI FRANKFORT: Excavator and art historian. A bit on the mystic side, but always stimulating and vital.

GORDON CHILDE: Archaeologist and historian, who believed firmly that "man made himself"—a good antidote to Frankfort.

M. E. MALLOWAN: "The man from Nimrud"—a thoroughgoing excavator primarily of northern Mesopotamia.

LEONARD WOOLLEY: "The man from Ur"—one of the great excavators of the ancient Near East, but prone to risky speculation.

ROBERT BRAIDWOOD: Pioneer prehistorian of the ancient Near East; to the archaeologist, he preached that a mud hovel says as much as a gilded palace.

H. C. RAWLINSON: Father of Assyriology; superb copyist, decipherer and organizer.

CARSTEN NIEBUHR: The Danish mathematician whose copies of Persepolis inscriptions started the cuneiform ball rolling.

G. F. GROTEFERD: The first serious decipherer of the cuneiform script.

EDWARD HINCKS: The brilliant "armchair" Irish scholar, who, with Rawlinson and Appert, formed the dedicated triad of cuneiform decipherment.

JULES APPERT: The distinguished French scholar who brought the words Sumer and Sumerians to the modern world.

SAMUEL NOAH KRAMER: "Mr. Sumerian Literature and Myth."

A. H. LAYARD: "The Englishman from Nineveh"—discoverer of the great Ashurbanipal library.

P. E. BOTTA: Layard's great French contemporary and counterpart; discoverer of the Assyrian palace at Khorsabad.

FRANCOIS THUREAU-DANGIN: France's most distinguished cuneiformist, who dominated the Assyriological scene for half a century.

ARNO POEBEL: Author of the first comprehensive and trustworthy Sumerian grammar.

ANTON DEIMEL: The Jesuit priest who compiled the most useful Sumerian glossary to date.

BENNO LANDSBERGER: The keenest mind in Assyriology in general, and cuneiform lexical studies in particular.

THORBILD JACOBSEN: Excavator, explorer and profound interpreter of Mesopotamian history and culture.

ADAM FALKENSTEIN: Founder of the highly productive Heidelberg school of cuneiform research.

FOR FURTHER READING

COTTRELL, LEONARD, *The Quest for Sumer*. New York, Putnam, 1965.
    Land of the Two Rivers. Cleveland, World, 1962.

FAIRSERVIS, WALTER A., JR., *Mesopotamia, the Civilization That Rose Out of Clay*. New York, Macmillan, 1964.

FAWCETT, RAYMOND, ed., *How Did They Live? Sumer*. Boston, Robert Bentley, n.d.

FEAGLES, ANITA, *He Who Saw Everything, the Epic of Gilgamesh*. New York, Scott, 1966.

MELLAART, JAMES, *Earliest Civilizations of the Near East*. New York, McGraw-Hill, 1965.

SAGGS, H. W. F., *Everyday Life in Babylonia and Assyria*. New York, Putnam, 1965.
    The Greatness That Was Babylon. New York, Hawthorne, 1962.

Reference sources: Beek, M. A., *Atlas of Mesopotamia*, London, 1962; *Cambridge Ancient History*, rev. ed., Cambridge, England, 1962; Chiera, Edward, *They Wrote on Clay*, 2d ed., Chicago, 1955; Cottrell, Leonard, *Lost Cities*, New York, 1963; Davidson, M. B., ed., *Horizon Book of the Lost Worlds*, New York, 1962; Frankfort, H., *The Art and Architecture of the Ancient Orient*, Baltimore, 1954; Frankfort, H., *The Birth of Civilization in the Near East*, New York, 1956; Frankfort, H., ed., *Intellectual Adventure of Ancient Man*, Chicago, 1946; Gelb, I. J., *Study of Writing: The Foundations of Grammatology*, Chicago, 1963; Gideion, S., *The Eternal Present*, Bollingen Series XXXV, 6, II; Goff, Beatrice Laura, *Symbols of Prehistoric Mesopotamia*, New Haven, and Woolley, Sir L., *The History of Mankind*, Vol. I, *Prehistory and the Beginnings of Civilization*, New York, 1963; Kraeling, C. H., and Adams, R. M., ed. *The City Invincible: A Symposium on Urbanization and Cultural Development in the Ancient Near East*, Chicago, 1960; Kramer, Samuel Noah, *Sumerian Mythology*, New York, 1961; Kramer, Samuel Noah, *History Begins at Sumer*, New York, 1959; Kramer, Samuel Noah, *The Sumerians: Their History, Culture and Character*, Chicago, 1963; Kramer, Samuel Noah, *Mesopotamia: The Cradle of Civilization*, New York, 1967; Lissner, Ivor, *The Living Past of 7000 Years of Civilization*, New York, 1957; Lloyd, Seton, *The Art of the Ancient Near East*, New York, 1961; Moscati, S., *The Face of the Ancient Orient*, New York, 1962; Muller, Herbert J., *The Loom of History*, Harper, 1958; Neugebauer, O., *The Exact Sciences in Antiquity*, Providence, 1957; Oppenheim, Leo, *Ancient Mesopotamia*, Chicago, 1964; Pallis, S. A., *The Antiquity of Iraq: A Handbook of Assyriology*, Copenhagen, 1956; Parrot, A., *Sumer: The Dawn of Art*, New York, 1961; Piggott, Stuart, ed., *The Dawn of Civilization*, New York, 1961; Pritchard, J. B., *Ancient Near Eastern Texts Relating to the Bible*, Princeton, 1955; Pritchard, J. B., *The Ancient Near East in Pictures*, Princeton, 1954; Saggs, H. W. F., *The Greatness That Was Babylon*, New York, 1962; Saggs, H. W. F., *Daily Life in Babylonia*, New York, 1965; Singer, C., and Holmyard, E. J., and Hall, A. R., *A History of Technology*, Oxford, 1956; Strommeyer, Eva, and Hirmer, Max, *5000 Years of the Art of Mesopotamia*, New York, 1956; Woolley, Sir Leonard, *Excavations at Ur*, London, 1955; Woolley, Sir Leonard, *Art of the Middle East*, New York, 1961. *Ur Excavations*, Vols. II, III, IV, V, X, University of Pennsylvania and the British Museum; *Illustrated London News*, selected issues, 1948–present.

INDEX

Entries in the Index that carry one asterisk* also appear in the Glossary. Entries that are marked with two asterisks** appear both in the Glossary and in the section on Gods, Demons, Cities. Italic numerals designate page reference to pictures.

Leonard Weisgard, author-artist of The Beginnings of Cities, has written and illustrated *The First Farmers* and *The Athenians* in the *Life Long Ago* series. Mr. Weisgard does extensive research in many scholarly sources to prepare the books. His striking illustrations are authentic in every detail, for he studies photographs of actual archaeological findings in planning them.

Dr. Samuel Noah Kramer, of the University of Pennsylvania Museum, has acted as Mr. Weisgard's archaeological adviser for The Beginnings of Cities. Dr. Kramer, a well-known archaeologist and author, is a noted authority on Sumerian culture. He has suggested a bibliography and checked the accuracy of the text and pictures.

Rosemary Daly, education consultant for the *Life Long Ago* series, has helped plan the entire book to make it of maximum use to readers and has prepared the Glossary and Index. Miss Daly is librarian of the Ethical Culture School in New York City.

Books in the *Life Long Ago* Series

The *Life Long Ago* books are closeup views of ancient civilizations. Everyday life is brilliantly re-created in panoramic scenes, authentic detailed drawings and concise text. Each book is a rare visual experience. Each takes the reader into the reality and excitement of history and provides an extraordinary understanding of a people and their ways.

THE BEGINNINGS OF CITIES

Pictures and Text by LEONARD WEISGARD

A vivid re-creation of the Mesopotamian world that built the first cities. You see the city grow from agricultural community into a center of trade and culture, developing art and architecture, religion, and methods of calculating and record keeping.

THE FIRST FARMERS in the New Stone Age

Pictures and Text by LEONARD WEISGARD

A striking pictorial treatment of one of the greatest revolutions in the history of man—the discovery of agriculture. You watch the earliest farmers at work—sowing grain, tending herds and making tools and pottery.

THE CAVE DWELLERS in the Old Stone Age

Pictures and Text by RICHARD M. POWERS

The pictures burst with life and strength. You feel the tense anticipation of the hunters as they gather before the magician in the ritual cave. You know the fear as they face a live mammoth, and realize they must kill or be killed.

THE EGYPTIANS in the Middle Kingdom

Pictures by SHANE MILLER
Text by EDWARD OCHSENSCHLAGER

A fascinating trip through this ancient land, where you will visit the lonely Pharaoh of Egypt, walk through the shop-lined streets of Memphis and journey past the Great Pyramids of Giza.

THE ROMANS in the Days of the Empire

Pictures and Text by SHANE MILLER

The mighty Roman Empire comes alive in the strength of these pictures. You take your seat at the Colosseum, you visit a Roman home, and you see the great Roman army prepare for battle.

THE ATHENIANS in the Classical Period

Pictures and Text by LEONARD WEISGARD

The beauty and reality of Athens are before you in the streets of the city as you visit an instrument maker's shop, join the crowds at the Panathenaic Stadium and stand before the Parthenon.